GET THEIR NAME

Workbook

GET THEIR NAME

Workbook

Grow Your Church
by Building New Relationships

KAY KOTAN

KEN WILLARD

Abingdon Press™

Nashville

GET THEIR NAME: WORKBOOK

ISBN 978-1-4267-8206-0

13 14 15 16 17 18 19 20 21 22—10 9 8 7 6 5 4 3 2 1

MANUFACTURED IN THE UNITED STATES OF AMERICA

PRAISE FOR
GET THEIR NAME

I thank God for the gift of this book! In an intensely practical way, the authors offer Christians training in evangelistic faith sharing that is grace-filled. Using a school-based metaphor, they help grow true Wesleyan evangelistic witness and faithfulness with a model that is applicable in virtually every church setting! I enthusiastically recommend *Get Their Name* for use in both lay and clergy training.

> —Bishop Mike Lowry, Bishop of the Central Texas Conference of the
> United Methodist Church

Get Their Name touches a nerve, intentionally! It teaches proven techniques for reaching people who are not yet connected to the church. Even more important, it will light a fire under clergy and laity, stimulating creative ideas to penetrate the mission fields of their own respective churches.

> —Jim Ozier, New Church Development & Congregational Transformation, North
> Texas Conference, UMC

This is a must-read resource for people who want to multiply their congregation's impact. Cultivating dynamic relationships with our neighbors is an urgent challenge for today's churches. *Get Their Name* is a practical, interactive guide that provides a map for building such relationships with those who are not yet in our church. The authors keep it simple, focused, and practical as they coax deeper faith-sharing and relationship-building that will result in life change for all. Grow your people as you grow God's kingdom by following the advice in this book.

> —Paul Nixon and Christie Latona, Founders of Readiness360.org

"People will not come until we first go." Sometimes, it is the basic reminders that stop us in our tracks and remind us we need an assessment. Bob, Doug, and Kay remind us of the need for intentional, missional plans for our lives and churches. Finally, they give us practical tools for engaging with the world around us and sharing the Good News in straightforward, doable actions!

> —Rev. Karen Koons Hayden, Director of Pastoral Excellence,
> Missouri Conference, UMC

CONTENTS

USING THIS WORKBOOK

This participant workbook is intended to be used as a companion to the book, *Get Their Name* by Bob Farr, Doug Anderson and Kay Kotan.

The goal of this workbook is to better enable you and your church to apply the key principles from the book.

Each of the ten sessions in this workbook corresponds directly to a chapter in the book.

While this workbook has been designed for group study, it can also be useful for individuals wishing to go deeper.

Group study sessions (for example: Sunday School classes, small groups, leadership teams, etc.) are designed to last 60-90 minutes.

Our intention is for the group to spend a week on each session. That would give everyone a week to read each of the ten chapters in the book and then meet together to go through the corresponding session. This is meant only as a guide. You and your group may read the whole book first, combine some sessions, spend more or less time on each session, whatever you choose. The focus should be on doing what will work best for your group.

A facilitator guide is available for download at:

www.GetTheirName.com

HERE ARE SOME BEST PRACTICES:

- Gather a team at your church to complete this study, then develop a plan to roll it out church-wide (such as an all-church study).

- Consider hiring a credentialed coach to help guide, support and hold the church leadership accountable for plan implementation (contact Kay Kotan at Kay@KayKotan.com if you need help finding a coach).

- Consider creating an ongoing team to work this process with intentionality to continuously evaluate and improve how you can grow your church by building relationships.

- Follow up this group study with one based on the book *Renovate or Die* by Bob Farr and Kay Kotan.

- Contact Ken Willard (Ken@L4T.org) about leading your team through a webinar leadership development session and/or coming to your church to hold a live leadership development workshop.

INTRODUCTION

Before we get into all of the specific sessions, it would be helpful for you to individually reflect on and respond to the following questions:

What are your personal beliefs about evangelism?

Where do you feel those beliefs come from?

How do you practice evangelism in your daily life?

How does your church practice evangelism?

How effective have you and your church been in reaching new people for Jesus Christ?

Review the four observations on page X in the book, *Get Their Name.*

Do you agree or disagree with these observations? Why?

What is your take-away from this reflection? If you are comfortable in doing so, share this with your group.

FAITH SHARING IN SERVICE

"Therefore, go and make disciples of all nations, baptizing them in the name of the Father and of the Son and of the Holy Spirit, teaching them to obey everything that I've commanded you. Look, I myself will be with you every day until the end of this present age."

Matthew 28:19-20

KEY POINTS:

- Our church beliefs and practices have led to the drastic decline in people connected to our church.

- Evangelism = Building authentic relationships with people we don't already know.

- Equipping people for evangelism requires an intentional process developed over time.

- Good Deed + Good Word = Good News

- Relational evangelism through service is connecting service to a clear communication of the Good News of God's love.

- We must meet people where THEY ARE not where WE ARE.

Other key points from this chapter:

PERSONAL REFLECTION

How have I been intentionally practicing servant evangelism?

How does our congregation practice servant evangelism?

How can the service I have been doing and in which our church is involved be shifted into relational evangelism?

GROUP DISCUSSION

Possible relational evangelism through service activities our church could consider:

1.

2.

3.

What training or resourcing might be needed to prepare for these?

GROUP DISCUSSION, CONTINUED

How might we say, "God loves you" through these elementary relational evangelism activities?

What activity are we doing now as a church fundraiser that might be changed into servant evangelism?

What changes need to be made?

PERSONAL JOURNEY

My key learning from today:

My next step:

FAITH SHARING IN GROUPS

"Come close and listen, all you who honor God; I will tell you what God has done for me: My mouth cried out to him with praise on my tongue."

Psalm 66:16

KEY POINTS:

- Faith sharing in groups begins with asking one another, "How have you experienced God in your life recently?"

- We must first find our own story.

- Practice your story in a safe place.

- Just playing church is no longer acceptable.

- Our faith must be grounded in a personal relationship with Jesus Christ that we regularly experience in transforming, life-giving ways that we share with others.

Other key points from this chapter:

PERSONAL REFLECTION

When have I been able to share my story with others at church in a small group setting?

Under what circumstances am I most comfortable sharing my story?

What keeps me from sharing my story with others? What am I willing to do to overcome those challenges?

GROUP DISCUSSION

What difference would it make for us to practice faith sharing in small groups at our church?

What are some benefits of faith sharing in small groups?

1.

2.

3.

GROUP DISCUSSION, CONTINUED

How might our church begin to incorporate faith sharing into our existing small groups?

How might our group encourage us to share how we have encountered God recently?

PERSONAL JOURNEY

My key learning from today:

My next step:

FAITH SHARING IN WORSHIP

"I will declare your name to my brothers and sisters; I will praise you in the very center of the congregation!"

Psalm 22:22

KEY POINTS:

- Faith sharing in worship builds upon faith sharing in groups.

- Faith sharing is best when it starts with our leaders.

- We need to offer consistent faith-sharing stories during our worship services.

- "Effective postmodern ministry is not only experiential, but also participatory." – Leonard Sweet, *The Church of the Perfect Storm*

Other key points from this chapter:

PERSONAL REFLECTION

When have I heard someone share their story in a worship service?

How did that feel? Was it connected to the message that day?

What part of my spiritual journey would I be most open to sharing in worship?

GROUP DISCUSSION

What's the difference between someone's testimony and their faith-sharing message?

What two steps need to occur before someone is typically prepared for faith sharing in worship?

GROUP DISCUSSION, CONTINUED

When has our church had members of the congregation share their faith in worship? Have we been consistent?

What might we do to engage more people in faith sharing in worship? What obstacles might we need to overcome first?

PERSONAL JOURNEY

My key learning from today:

My next step:

FAITH SHARING WITH THE UNCONNECTED

"The master said to the servant, 'Go to the highways and back alleys and urge people to come so that my house will be filled.'"

Luke 14:23

KEY POINTS:

- An invitation should be personal, specific, and part of your relationship with that person.

- Special Sundays and/or special events provide the congregation a reason to invite someone new.

- Relationship should always come before an invitation.

Other key points from this chapter:

PERSONAL REFLECTION

Who was the last person I invited to a specific worship service at my church?

What keeps me from inviting people I already know to attend a worship service at our church?

Who do I already know (family, close friends, co-worker, neighbor, etc.) that I would be willing to invite to a worship service in the next three months?

Who might I invest time with to build a relationship that would lead to an authentic invitation?

GROUP DISCUSSION

How did we come to this church? [born here, married into it, parents brought us, were invited, etc.]

How many guests do we have in church each weekend?

What can we do to create more opportunities for people to invite others to worship?

GROUP DISCUSSION, CONTINUED

What special worship service do we have already on the calendar that can be turned into an "Invitation Worship?"

Where is our group today? [elementary, middle school, high school, college evangelism]

What is our next step to move toward the next level?

PERSONAL JOURNEY

My key learning from today:

My next step:

GROUP LEARNINGS FROM SESSION ONE

1. Faith Sharing in Service

2. Faith Sharing in Groups

3. Faith Sharing in Worship

4. Faith Sharing with the Unconnected

GROUP NEXT STEPS

What will our group commit to doing based on what we have learned in the previous section?

BEGINNING OUTSIDE CONVERSATIONS

"You are the light of the world. A city on top of a hill can't be hidden."

Matthew 5:14

KEY POINTS:

- Without an intentional plan for becoming missional, we risk living our lives as secularly as those who have never experienced God.

- Every church has two mission fields.

- It is important for us to count the describe-ables.

- Since we no longer live in a church-centric culture, we must be more intentional than ever in placing ourselves in opportunities to meet people and share our story.

- We must learn about the culture in our church's mission field.

- We are going to have to sacrifice some of our preferences and likes in order to reach unconnected people with different preferences and likes.

- Engage the radar so as not to miss opportunities to start conversations.

- God works best through our natural settings (affinities).

- Evangelism is more of an art than a science. It is not about selling.

- We are ALL called to be missionaries.

Other key points from this chapter:

PERSONAL REFLECTION

What is the one thing I don't ever want to see changed at our church?

Where can I intentionally get out of my "Christian bubble" to engage my radar and start conversations?

Who have I seen model starting a conversation with someone new?

GROUP DISCUSSION

Which mission field (the connected or the unconnected) is our church most focused on today? Why?

Step One – Have an Intentional Plan

Step Two – Set a Daily Goal

Step Three – Build Trust

Step Four – Mutual Respect

Step Five – The Conversation

Step Six – Become a Model

What step comes most naturally to you? Why do you think that is true?

GROUP DISCUSSION, CONTINUED

What step is the most challenging? Why?

How might our church better equip the congregation in these steps?

What would accountability look like for implementing these steps in our church?

PERSONAL JOURNEY

My key learning from today:

My next step:

CREATING OPPORTUNITIES FOR NEW RELATIONSHIPS

"Act wisely toward outsiders, making the most of the opportunity. Your speech should always be gracious and sprinkled with insight so that you may know how to respond to every person."

Colossians 4:5-6

KEY POINTS:

- We must begin to focus more of our time, resources and relationships on those not yet connected to the church instead of only on those who are already here.

- Pastors and laity leaders need to focus on the important and not just on the urgent.

- Our business is people and Jesus, and Jesus and people. Our mission should be to build a bridge between the two.

- We must build a culture of expectation and experimentation.

Other key points from this chapter:

PERSONAL REFLECTION

Where are my normal affinities? Where do I like to hang out locally?

Which of the eight strategies listed in this chapter do I find the most appealing? Why?

How would I feel if our pastor was spending a little more time in the community and a little less time with us?

GROUP DISCUSSION

1) Work Within Your Normal Affinities

2) Member-Guest Events (Church)

3) Work Outside Your Comfort Zone

4) Create Margins in Your Life

5) Routine Introductions and Handing Out Business Cards

6) Create Hangout Places

7) Slow Down and Offer Blessings

8) Organization Connection Strategies

If the business of our church is people and Jesus . . . How's business?

Which of the eight strategies listed above should our group focus on next? Why?

GROUP DISCUSSION, CONTINUED

How might our church equip more people to create opportunities to build new relationships?

What would accountability look like in this new strategy?

PERSONAL JOURNEY

My key learning from today:

My next step:

MOVING FROM ACQUAINTANCE TO AUTHENTIC RELATIONSHIP

"…I will also appoint you as a light to the nations so that my salvation may reach to the end of the earth."

Isaiah 49:6b

KEY POINTS:

- We must connect and build relationships with unconnected people.

- A key factor in building relationships is to build trust.

- It takes time, perseverance and intentionality to move from an acquaintance to an authentic relationship.

- We have to make room in our lives to build new relationships with unconnected people.

- The more we practice the process, the easier and more natural it will become.

Other key points from this chapter:

PERSONAL REFLECTION

How does it feel when someone is trying to sell me something?

In a conversation with someone, which comes more natural to me: listening or talking?

When did I last notice God putting someone new in front of me somewhere? How did I respond?

GROUP DISCUSSION

Step One: Listen for Their Story

Step Two: Watch for Signals

Step Three: Bridge-Building Phrases

Step Four: Know Your Elevator Story

- Why God?

- Why Church?

- Why My Church?

Step Five: Knowing Your Faith Story

Step Six: Find the Need and Connect New People with New People

How easy is it for us to listen to someone else's story without telling ours?

What do we think the unconnected in our community know about our church?

GROUP DISCUSSION, CONTINUED

Why does our community need our church?

How might our church connect more new people with other new people (instead of asking them to join with those who have been here for a long time)?

PERSONAL JOURNEY

My key learning from today:

My next step:

GROUP LEARNINGS FROM SESSION TWO

5. Beginning Outside Conversations

6. Creating Opportunities for New Relationships

7. Moving from Acquaintance to Authentic Relationship

GROUP NEXT STEPS

What will our group commit to doing based on what we have learned in the previous section?

LEADERSHIP MATTERS

"Rely on your leaders and defer to them, because they watch over your whole be-ing as people who are going to be held responsible for you. They need to be able to do this with pleasure and not with complaints about you, because that wouldn't help you."

Hebrews 13:17

KEY POINTS:

- The number one roadblock for connected people inviting unconnected people to worship is that they are not confident in the experience guests will have when they arrive.

- To reach unconnected new people, we must develop a new culture.

- We are friendly . . . to each other.

- Three needed "wows": radical hospitality, music ministry, and children's ministry.

- The greatest gift the church has to give away is relationship.

- Radical hospitality is not meeting but exceeding expectations.

- Relationship Trinity = God + others + availability

- The purpose of a church is to create new disciples of Jesus Christ for the transformation of the world.

- We must do strategic ministry planning and evaluating on a continual and consistent basis.

- Churches must equip their leaders for ministry. Our church will only grow as fast as we can raise up new leaders.

- Got to preach it 'til you see it!

- Everyone is responsible for hospitality.

Other key points from this chapter:

PERSONAL REFLECTION

What am I currently doing to ensure radical hospitality at our church?

What type of experience do I think a first-time guest would really have at our church?

What if she were a 20-something single mother?

GROUP DISCUSSION

How does our church plan and evaluate our ministries? Has that been effective in determining the best use of our resources? What should we do if a ministry is no longer growing or helping us to make disciples?

What process are we using to identify and raise up new leaders? What steps would be helpful for us to add to our current leadership development?

Are we as friendly to those we don't know as to those who have been here for years?

GROUP DISCUSSION, CONTINUED

1   2   3   4   5   6   7   8   9   10

No   Basic   Radical
Hospitality   Hospitality   Hospitality

Where does our church currently fall? Why?

What would be a good next step for us to take as a church to move us up the scale?

PERSONAL JOURNEY

My key learning from today:

My next step:

YOUR BUILDING MATTERS

"You are the body of Christ and parts of each other."

1 Corinthians 12:27

KEY POINTS:

- Don't leave the connection process to chance! It must be intentional.

- We must build a culture of hospitality, not just a hospitality team.

- Prepare for guests every time the door opens.

Other key points from this chapter:

PERSONAL REFLECTION

When was a time I found myself in an environment where I did not understand what was going on, or maybe felt lost about where to go?

How does it feel when I'm in a very unfamiliar situation and/or environment?

Guests are coming to your home next week. What would you do to prepare?

GROUP DISCUSSION

Once a new person comes to a worship service at our church, where are they most likely to connect into the life of our church? Why?

Hospitality Checklist

1. Exterior Signage and Accessibility

2. First Impression of Human Hospitality

3. How to Get Their Names

4. Think Guest, Not Visitor

5. Connector

6. Welcome Center

7. Lobby

8. Nursery

9. Pre-Worship Atmosphere

10. Meet and Greet

11. Announcements

12. Worship Participation

13. After-Worship Experience

14. Hire Mystery Worshipers

15. Improve Your Social Media Presence and Impression

16. Critical Mass

GROUP DISCUSSION, CONTINUED

In which three items on the checklist is our church the strongest?

Which three items on the checklist does our church need to focus on next?

What can our group do next to help in one of these areas?

PERSONAL JOURNEY

My key learning from today:

My next step:

RELATIONSHIPS MATTER

"This is right and it pleases God our savior, who wants all people to be saved and to come to a knowledge of the truth."

1 Timothy 2:3-4

KEY POINTS:

- Friendliness is not enough. People are searching for relationships.

- We must have an intentional process to move people from outsider to guest, from guest to connected, from connected to disciple, from disciple to missionary.

- Bridge events are the best way to get out of the church and build relationships with those in our mission field using non-threatening methods.

- Make new people a priority.

- We must have an intentional faith development process.

- Move people toward becoming ambassadors for Christ.

Other key points from this chapter:

PERSONAL REFLECTION

What am I willing to give up? How uncomfortable am I willing to be? What do I love about our church that I'm willing to see changed in order to reach more people for Jesus Christ?

For whom or for what do I usually pray?

For whom or for what am I feeling led to add to my prayers?

GROUP DISCUSSION

What events is our church currently doing that might be considered Bridge Events?

What event have we done or what event are we planning that might be adjusted to become a real Bridge Event?

What would be a good Bridge Event for our church to do next year? What are the next steps we need to take to host this event?

GROUP DISCUSSION, CONTINUED

What does the connection process look like in our church?

How might our church better connect first-time guests and others into the life of our church?

What could our group do to help our church better connect people into the church?

GROUP DISCUSSION, CONTINUED

What is the current discipleship pathway for faith development in our church (children and adults)?

Is that pathway effective? How do we know?

What should our church do in order to strengthen that process?

GROUP DISCUSSION, CONTINUED

What can our group do to help?

Who are the ambassadors for Christ in our church? Are they mentoring others?

How can those of us in this group become better ambassadors?

PERSONAL JOURNEY

My key learning from today:

My next step:

GROUP LEARNINGS FROM SESSION THREE

8. Leadership Matters

9. Your Building Matters

10. Relationships Matter

GROUP NEXT STEPS

What will our group commit to doing based on what we have learned in the previous section?

CPSIA information can be obtained at www.ICGtesting.com
Printed in the USA
LVOW08s1502250713

344651LV00027B/1389/P